MW00896563

12 Rounds to Winning for the Youth

By Evan Holyfield

ISBN 13:
9781794605237
Copyright © 2019 by Evan Holyfield

All rights reserved. This book or any portion thereof
may not be reproduced or used in any manner whatsoever
without the express written permission of the publisher.

Printed in the United States of America

Cover Photo by Herman Rodriguez

With Inita Callaway and Toi Irvin
For Publishing Advantage Group

Published By:
Publishing Advantage Group
www.publishingadvantagegroup.com

Contents

Foreword

I really believe what the word of God says, "We go from glory to glory." Each generation gets better. I tell my son that he doesn't need to drink or smoke, because these are the things that can hinder him athletically. I encourage him to not let relationships distract him from pursuing his goals and to try to avoid conflicts when he is preparing for fights. **Success is a plan, so you must plan to win.** As parents we have to ask ourselves, what are we going to do for our kids to succeed? I believe he can make it because I made it. I made it because it was a plan. My father wasn't involved in my life to encourage me, so my old trainer told me that I could make it and I believed him after I got an ok from my mom. **In order for me to be successful at boxing I had to listen, follow directions and not quit.**

My mom wouldn't let me get distracted from my goals, especially when I was at the Boys and Girls Club. I think that these are the things that parents want to do to keep their kids focused. You do this when they are young so that when they are older, they can remember to focus. A lot of success has to do with the parents and what the parents are telling their kids. If it worked for me why shouldn't it work for my son?

As an amateur boxer, Evan can be the very best, he will continue to develop. Evan is 20 years old, he is on the right track and he is even stronger than I was at that age. I didn't have to go through what he is going through. Everybody is looking forward to beating him up. When I was boxing, no one knew who I was, and they didn't care if I fought them. I came up a light heavyweight and took over the whole thing. Everybody already knows who Evan is, he can't sneak up on nobody. He is developing to be great. Evan's body is just like mine, when I was 20, my shoulders were wider, my legs were about the same size, but one thing I can say is that my thighs were bigger than his. My friends said my legs were so skinny that if I broke my legs, they were going to have to shoot me. But one thing my friends knew was that I was strong. When I was a kid, I was told that my daddy was strong, so that's why I never let nobody outwork me. I tell my son, throw more punches; that means you outworking this guy. If he throws a punch, you throw one more. That's the whole big thing about outworking somebody; I'm going to do a little bit more. **Always believe that you can do a little bit more.**

My mom told me to not worry about nothing, life ain't about worrying, it's about doing things. Do the best that you can do and be the best that you can be. I think Evan should not be concerned about the opinions of other people comparing him to me because every day is a new day; good or bad will chase you the next day. When people judge him, they don't realize that he isn't finished. Most of those people probably didn't get to watch me fight amateur. Evan isn't a pro yet. He is a work in progress and in even so much I can say he is as good as me when I was 19 and 20.

When it comes to who he is hanging around, I always tell him that some of your friends don't even fight, they are majoring in business. If you don't make it into boxing, they are going to be better than you because you have been practicing boxing and they have been studying business. Boxing is your first.

I wanted to make enough money where my mom wouldn't have to ask for money from nobody, I saw my mom get upset because people didn't do their part. I told her she wasn't going to have to worry about nothing, I was going to help her, so in 1984 I was able to do it, my mom died in 1996. I took care of her so that she never had to worry about bills. That was my goal as a kid for who I loved the most. Nothing was dear to me but my mom and grandmama.

Evander Holyfield

Introduction

True champions are not created overnight. The unrelenting makings of a champion are confidence, hard work, a winner's mindset, sacrifice, integrity, and heart. I was thrusted into my first boxing match, with no prior training, besides the sparring I had done with my father. On the outside, my small 8-year-old frame did not look ready for this fight, but on the inside, there was a different story being told. One of a fearless heart and winners' mentality, that no one could see just by looking at me. The cliché "never judge a book by its cover" definitely applied this day. You can never know someone's full potential until they show you. As I got older and tried to recall some of the details, the only thing I can remember is that I wanted to win. I wanted to be the victor and I was determined to give it my all. I really did not have a choice. Either I stand there and get hit or fight back; so, I chose the latter, I chose to fight back. Once I gloved up, I knew I had to fight to win. My dad told me I needed to throw the most punches and that's what I did. He told me to keep moving forward and not let the other guy back me into the ropes. With those directions, I won my fight. His advice was just as important as my mouth guard, gloves, shorts, and shoes. Although I won the fight, it was an unexpected win because I was the quiet or sweet kid as my mom would describe me and of course many people judging a book by its cover. Becoming a champion starts way before the accomplishments, accolades, or recognitions are received. We will talk about mindset in depth within the rounds. Transforming into a champion begins in your mind first, believing you can win starts with you. "I *am the greatest, I said that before I even knew I was.*" – Muhammad Ali

As an amateur boxer, I fight three rounds at three minutes each. That totals nine minutes and translates into 530 seconds. I have 530 seconds to outwit my opponent for the win; boxing is a thinking man's sport. Most people think that a muscle filled body, strong neck, and fast feet are the requirements to be a boxer, but that is furthest from the truth. The mindset of a boxer or any champion is the key. The punches and fancy footwork are the caveat, but all of the winning starts in the mind. Anyone can train to be strong physically but can that same person be trained to have a strong mind; which is where all winning starts.

Before any match I perform a ritual. My game rituals are what I like to call the four P's: **Prayer, Peace, Painting** the picture, and **Preparing** for the win. I will talk about this more inside of the rounds. Each champion needs a ritual. Start to think about your specific ritual to preparing for the win. This winner's mentality has already taken me on the track to currently being the number one amateur boxer in Georgia. My next path is-becoming a professional champion of the world. Is this road easy? By no means. Is this road worth it? Indeed, it is. You see how I already claimed my destination, middle weight boxing champion of the world. I speak with power and conviction. My words have power and so does yours. I believe that, and I can see it. By the time you get to the last round of this book, maybe you will be worn out, sweat beads streaming down your face with a swollen left eye, and hints of blood in your teeth; you kept fighting because you have the conqueror's mindset. You too will see the destination of your dreams and how each step you make will be another step in that direction. The goal of this book is to illustrate through what I know and love, boxing, on how to win, overcome and be a champion in any profession, through any obstacle that the youth may experience. This book will display my personal struggles through boxing and experiences out of the ring. My prayer is that you learn from them. We are all different, but one thing is for certain, the formula to winning is similar and through the twelve rounds of this book, you too will learn how to have a champion's mindset. In pro boxing, there are twelve rounds and each round will prepare you for the next round of winning. Are you willing to fight to win and chase your dreams? From the workouts, pressure, unexpected jabs, to the people in your corner and everything in between, there is a winner ready to be made. You will be completely transformed, and I am looking forward to it. Champions do not leave any dreams on the table, follow your dreams and put in the hard work to accomplish them.

I, Evan Holyfield, will serve as your trainer through this match. We will walk this road together learning as we win together. We are pushing towards our dreams together. Every boxer needs a trainer and/or a team. My trainer and team do an excellent job coaching me through those difficult times and I will pay it forward and provide the same service for you.

To make this a practical book for learning, I included advice at the end of each round called, "contender's corner". The contender is the person you are fighting to win the championship against [or whatever you are aspiring towards] the corner is the corner of the boxing ring [life] that you have to get in to regroup and get ready for the next round. Each "contender's corner" message will build upon the last preparing you for the 12th round. In the 12th round, you will have all the tools needed to knockout your opponent [or obstacles/challenges] and become the champion I know is living inside of you.

To drive home some points and create the best experience possible, I have included some history about the sport of boxing that will add another layer to this journey you are about to take. I also enlisted help, through quotes from some of the tremendous boxers that have reigned before me and have laid the groundwork for a young boxer like myself coming up in the rinks. My father is included, yes, my father, the undisputed four-time heavyweight champion of the world, Evander the Real Deal Holyfield! "*People who make the choice to study, work hard or whatever they endeavor to do is to give it the max on themselves to reach the top level. And you have the people who get envious and jealous, yet are not willing to put that work in, and they want to get the same praise.*" Evander Holyfield

Let's go novice it is time to glove up!

Ding, Ding. Ding!

Let's get ready to rummmmmbbbbllle!

Round 1

Round 1:

Discipline

How Disciplined Are You?

"Anyone will succeed in whatever field of endeavor in life by acquiring the same virtues and character that boxing world champions do – dedication, perseverance, courage, extreme self-discipline and prayers."
– Manny Pacquiao

Picture waking up at 5:30 AM daily to conquer a strenuous two-hour workout, only to get prepared for two more strenuous workouts later in the day, for another two to three intense hours. The average person would frown at such a task much like you probably did when you read that. My training also includes a taxing seven mile run up, down and around Stone Mountain in Georgia. Let me tell you about the famous Stone Mountain. This mountain is over 1,600 feet tall and is a two-mile round trip up. If you run around this intimidating mountain you will have added another five miles. I respect the climb because it reminds me of my fights. I always approach this mountain with humility, respect, caution and confidence. Like my run up Stone Mountain, I feel the same sense of accomplishment when I complete a match. This is my grueling schedule, and this is what makes my day complete.

Most days I have to get up at 5 AM. This is when the true

test of your discipline either sinks or swims. My personal definition of discipline is pushing through when things get tough and having the mindset to finish what you started by giving 100% commitment every day. When my legs start to feel as heavy as cement blocks, all I can do is dig deep to keep moving when my physical body wants to quit. My body feels like it has been pushed to its very limit. At this point my discipline starts and this is where my training and determination come in hand. I then will pray and ask God for strength to keep pushing. Our strength only goes so far, like a short jab, but God is the one who can extend the jab to be successful. The things my parents had me doing as a child prepared me for the discipline I have for boxing. My mother, like any mother, wanted the best for me and did everything she could to make sure I was staying active and productive six days a week. On the outside looking in, it seemed like all I did was play sports, train, and study hard. It was true, I worked extremely hard and learned great lessons about being accountable for my own actions. Any sport you can name, I have probably had the pleasure of learning and training for it since the age of two.

Initially, my mom intentionally steered me away from boxing. Track, basketball, swimming, martial arts, gymnastics and even football were the sports I competed in. Participating in sports filled a lot of my early childhood and academia filled what was left. I studied foreign languages, like Japanese and Spanish. I attended a multitude of educational centered events such as museums and theatres, plays, musicals, events around the world and by the time I was three years old I was reading because of it. Through all of the different coaches and sports I played, I absorbed little things from everyone and made them my own. The habits I established at an early age laid the foundation of my life as a disciplined young man.

My first match at the age of eight showed me that I could actually fight and hold my own. It also showed me how comfortable I was boxing. Before I had to glove up to fight, I had never set foot in a ring; my mother did a pretty good job of keeping me shielded from the sport, as best she could. It is kind of difficult to keep yourself away from the sport when your father is a four-time heavyweight champion of the world. Spectators were sure this would be an easy win for my opponent, but I won the fight with no prior training. Simple sparring with my father right before the match was the only real training I had received. The discipline that I had acquired from years prior prepared me for the match and my agility from the workouts helped my stamina. My mother was still not convinced this was something that was right for me, even though I was victorious, it was like the instinct to fight and win was natural. When you are looking to be disciplined in one area of your life, there is usually evidence in other parts of your life that will determine how successful you will be, no matter what the task. What are your habits? Are they conducive to your discipline?

My Childhood Shaped My Discipline

From the age of eight to twelve, when I was not in the ring, I practiced martial arts. Instead of kicking, as the sport requires, I threw more punches, as it was a natural instinct for me. While competing for the martial arts nationals I lost the match because I hit my opponent too hard with my fist. After that experience, I decided to pursue amateur boxing so that I could throw as many force-filled punches as I wanted without getting points deducted. I battled with myself to suppress the passion for boxing, although it was already part of my DNA. At this point I didn't want to leave my dreams on the table. In boxing, that can be compared to getting sucker punched because you were focused on something else instead of your dreams. One day I went to my mom and told her I wanted to let all the other sports go and focus in on boxing. She reluctantly allowed me to choose my own path to greatness, that was at 12 years old. At the time, I was playing football and I abruptly let that go to train and learn the art of boxing exclusively. To prove to her how serious I was, I would get up at the crack of dawn to be at CrossFit training at 5AM, on my own, and ride my skateboard there. All this took place before school, and then after school I would practice for two hours, come home for tutoring, eat and crash and do it all over again the next day. Not to mention the Saturday training I had to accomplish. My mom told me the neighbors were impressed by my work ethic and how dedicated I was at such a young age. They watched how persistent and consistent I was with training early mornings before school by riding my skateboard to practice in the dark. The neighbors then began enrolling their own kids in CrossFit. This was my entire middle and high school career routine. I trained about 365 days a year, there was no such thing as time off. The burning desire inside to succeed outweighed thoughts of doubt in my mind, so working hard was no problem for me.

Once I began training for the sport and learning the art of boxing full time, I became closer to mastering my craft and reaching my goals of becoming a top ranked amateur boxer and champion. My hunger to win went into overdrive.

Boxing reintroduced some key ideas for me that I had been

exposed to within other sports and taught me things that I did not know. Most people think that boxing is just throwing punches and trying to protect your face. This is a component, but it is just the surface. Boxing requires, speed, agility, power, finesse, endurance, and the greatest skill, mental toughness. Boxing is a thinking man's sport. You have to exercise your mind just as much as your body. The mind leads where the body goes. You have to learn how to figure out your opponent's weakness rather quickly. Many people assume boxing is for the angry, but it is the total opposite. Boxing is for the one who can control their emotions and calm down to think strategically on their next move. Any sudden movements can be an opportunity for your opponent to find a weakness in you and go in for the win. Just like in life when you are faced with certain issues, you have to possess mental strength to get through it. It is easy to buckle under pressure if your mind is not on board. Boxing teaches that mental strength and discipline is just as important as any punch you could ever throw.

Training as a boxer is very intense, but I always seemed to push through on my limited strength with God's help. My boxing trainers incorporated a workout that was swimming based. At the time, I did not know why because it was not the most favorable thing for me to do and my thought was: how exactly was this going to prepare me for a match? Now, I have taken swimming lessons as a child and it wasn't as intense as treading water several minutes. The workout included me treading water for twenty minutes straight. Treading water for several minutes is not a task for a novice swimmer. Treading water is maintaining an upright position in deep water by kicking the feet in a walking motion, while the hands are slightly cupped in a downward circular motion. Sounds tough, right? It can be, but its beneficial for a boxer to be able to master this skill because it is a lot like a match. If I would have stopped swimming I would have drowned. In boxing, if I stop throwing punches, I will lose the match. This an indicator of how the boxing match will be, so if I train like this, I will be successful during my matches. Even when my stamina is fading and I'm growing tired I have to remember I am fighting, and I need to press through to win.

When I feel like I want to take a day off from training or that I am tired during a workout and do not want to go on, I can hear my father's voice from my childhood just as clear as if he was standing next to me. "Son, no excuses!" My father has instilled the idea that without discipline one cannot achieve winning results. He is also big on doing things for yourself when no one is looking. Like grinding extra hard or running that extra mile. Are you going the extra mile when no one is looking? Most importantly, do you want to win? That is the ultimate question. Yes, the answer is YES!

The one other thing that keeps me focused or going besides my father's consistent and repetitive advice are my future fights and my team of trainers. Picturing myself standing in the ring, ready to fight my opponent, with winning on my mind: I have to think about the training I have done. The workouts I have completed. Did my opponent out train me? Did I do *everything* within my control to make sure I will be successful in this fight? How was my control this week? All of that goes back to how disciplined I was during my preparation towards my goal to win. Are you disciplined enough to win?

In life, we are faced with situations that require us to have discipline in one area in order to achieve winning results in another. For example, if you are striving to earn great grades in school, your discipline requires you to study so many hours of the day and work strategically for other ways to improve. What happens when you do not feel like reading another book or doing more research? What tools do you use to get you back focused? Think about it and hold that thought. Where are you investing your time? I always ask myself, "is this a great investment of my time?" Time is valuable and that is one thing we cannot retrieve, so being disciplined always requires you to invest your time wisely towards the efforts that will make you win in life. Remember, giving up is not an option. NO EXCUSES. When I think about quitting, I instantly think about my why. Your why is the purpose you are completing the task you are faced with. This helps you stay focused and persevere through your obstacle. My desire to be a great boxer and middle weight champion of the world is my why. Making my family proud of me is my why. You have to define your "why" or purpose in life and you will start to see other great things begin to manifest. Figuring out your "why" is important because it's what motivates you to not give up. Your why is your fire, it's your second wind. Your why is your zone and your zone is where the impossible becomes the possible.

Discipline is Necessary

What I have learned as an amateur boxer is that self-discipline is crucial. As you can see, this in not for the faint. In life, your challenges are going to come at you fast and hard and you need to know how to get up, keep going even when if it is uncomfortable, and you want to give up. Keep in mind, if you are not uncomfortable, you will not grow.

7

You have to push through the uncomfortable stage because positive and beneficial growth is on the other side. Always remember this, there is good on the other side, you can't quit now. You are almost there. I am in your corner just as my coach is in mine's. Take a sip of water, get a towel and dry your face. Now let's get it!

Contender's Corner

Without self-control or discipline it is difficult to reach your goals and stay at a certain level of success. I challenge you to tighten your gloves up and get in your boxing stance; we can work on improving your discipline. I saw a few jabs that could have been avoided had you been investing your time better. Always be aware and pay attention to the time you invest in anything. Round one, discipline, is the first principle you need to possess to master any goal. You were decent, but you have the potential to be great or undefeated. There will be times when you do not want to carry out your goals and your "why" will need to be clear to you, so you can muster up the strength to keep pushing. Just like in boxing, you have to work your footing, but not too much, and get a feel for your opponent so you know how to strategically get the win. We have 11 more rounds to go and I believe in your discipline and strength. These rounds are not easy, only the strong will survive. Think about these questions as we move through to the next round.

Focus on the questions below.

- Think about your "why" what keeps you motivated to keep going in life?

- What can you do each day that will serve as a

foundation for great work ethic and discipline moving forward?

Sparring is up next. This is the round that prepares you for the different techniques for the match. You have your structure and discipline, now let's go to the next level and spar to get better.

Round 2

Sparring

"Practice Makes Perfect"

Once that bell rings you're on your own. It's just you and the other guy." – Joe Lewis

Sparring is necessary and probably the single most important thing in boxing. Let's be clear, there is a distinction between sparring and fighting. Sparring is to help develop your skills while fighting is to destroy your opponent. It is a tool that is used to prepare you for real life instances, in whatever you are preparing for. In life, we are faced with obstacles that prepares us for the bigger fight that we will ultimately face. Imagine preparing for an important test by reading and doing practice questions or putting in laps and sprints for a track meet. These are your sparring sessions and you have the opportunity to fine tune your skills before it's time to perform. As youth, you must understand when you are being pruned or shaped for the win, like in sparring. The round we just ended, discipline, is beneficial to achieving anything in life and is not an easy principle for anyone but an essential one.

Life makes you think you are ready to crush your goals, but when an obstacle comes your way and it knocks you off your square, it's a direct reflection of your discipline. You either get up and push through or stay down and give up. I know you are a novice, but if you learn self-discipline early on you will be a better athlete. With that being said, sparring in boxing is your friend, your best friend. No boxer EVER has not sparred! Since you are a novice at this point, you will be sparring for the duration of your career. Sparring is a skill shaping idea. All your repetitive punches, your strategy, your weak points, your strong points, and your fancy footwork will fine tune you to become a great boxer. During sparring, you can correct them, but in a fight, you cannot. Sparring in life is practicing for those goals you are ready to achieve. Each thing you do prepares you for reaching your goals. Sparring is only useful if it is used to prepare for the future. Getting ready in life is only useful if you use what you learn and apply it, if not, that was time wasted. Us boxers use our sparring sessions to rehearse for the fight and to apply what was learned from the sparring sessions to the actual match. Let's not get ahead of ourselves, as a novice we have to ease into this. There are some steps I will talk to you about that will prepare you to actually full out spar. We need to take the correct provisions; I would not want you to get hurt under my direction. Same in life, you need to test the waters and get familiar with the goals before you get hurt. There is nothing like going after something that you are not properly prepared for; you will ultimately have to do it all over again. Now had you sparred and fine-tuned your approach your outcome would have been more favorable.

This round is set up so you do not have to work backwards. Working backwards means trying to step in the ring with no sparring practice. Only to get defeated because of your lack of knowledge and be forced to learn techniques about the sport the difficult way. Boxers work smart – remember, this is a thinking man's sport.

It is said that it takes 10,000 deliberate hours for a person to master a skill. If you are spending a vast amount of time in the ring sparring and mastering those different skills that you lack, eventually you will be a master at it. This is the reason why I spend countless hours in the gym training and sparring with other guys to master my skills. I set small goals to reach the ultimate goals I have set. When chasing after your personal goals, you must spend time in whatever it may be; practicing and preparing for it to become better.

Choosing Sparring Partners

We want to always have the best sparring partners, so they can bring out the best in us. If you are preparing for a test, you want to get a person with top notch skills in that area, so you can learn from them while correcting any of your mistakes along the way. It makes no sense to summon someone in life that is inexperienced to help you improve in any area of your journey, it is pointless and not helpful to becoming a champion. Here are a few tips before you begin looking at your opponent in the eye that are important. Always stare down your goals in life, no matter how big or small they may seem. Remember to BREATHE! Finally, get comfortable and have fun. Remember I will always set you up for success.

The following are a few key points that a novice boxer needs to practice in order to be relaxed in the ring before they actually do a full sparring session. Remember, being prepared is always key. Never go into any new challenge unprepared.

- ## Punching with a Trained Fighter

  I would not throw you in the ring without having ever fought. So, before we spar, boxers should practice just doing the one thing that makes the sport what it is, throwing punches. You will train and just throw them with an experienced boxer to get the hang of boxing. To get comfortable in the ring and to work on your stance, breathing techniques, defense and offense. Listen, I know you are pumped at this point and you are ready to knock down all your goals one at a time, but you need to practice with someone who has been on the road you want to travel. Give them your best swing at things and let them show you what to do to improve. Listen to those who have experience, experience is the best teacher.

- ## Shadowboxing

  The ring can look intimidating, but this is why we are practicing. Shadowboxing allows boxers to get in the ring and practice throwing punches, but none of the punches land on anyone. The boxers must practice throwing several combinations of punches; jabs, upper cuts, right hooks, etc. Throwing jabs at your goals allows you to outwork the opponent so that when you are faced with an opportunity to actually land a punch, you will be great. Practicing with yourself will help you envision what you want to do in the ring before the real thing.

- ## Catching Jabs

  This is what we have both been waiting for, the actual contact punch, but this is the lightest jab. Not to harm, but to practice the jabs. Move around a bit, see what is comfortable, see what works. Make sure you keep your balance too. There are a lot of components that work together to make the boxing experience what it is. Pay attention to your body and motion. When chasing down goals, this is like having a test run to get you prepared to master one level. By the time it is time to get to the next level, you will be prepared to throw jabs.

- ## Jab Drills

  This is where you can get more creative. You can start to craft jab punches, but you only get five, then it is time for your partner to throw some. This is how you get ready for strategizing in life, by trying different things to see what works or what should be shelved and developed more. Here is where you will build your arsenal of weaponry to pull out during the actual match or the actual goal you are working to crush.

- ## 1-2's

  Here we go, we are getting closer to actually sparring, but we have to be positive that you are ready to get in the ring and spar. Now we are getting down to the grit of things, you get to throw 1-2 punches and use combinations, with a max of 3 punches, so throw them wisely. I forgot to mention that you cannot use your right hand. No hooks or uppercuts are allowed either, remember we are not trying to hurt our partner. We are trying to get you, the novice fighter ready for sparring.

You are now ready to full on spar. Let's get it!

I see the apprehension in your eye, but rest assured, I have the full confidence that you will be a great boxer soon.

Professional Sparring

Floyd Mayweather [50 F 0 L] sparred with left-handed boxers to fine tune his skills while preparing for the 2017 match against Connor McGregor. Larry Holmes [75 F 69 W] was a sparring partner for Joe Frazier [37 F 32 W] and Muhmmad Ali [56 F 51 W]. See the trends, these fighters are all great boxers, with the exception of McGregor, he is a great UFC that wanted to box a professional boxer. The point is, they all sparred with someone who was as good or just as good as them, upgrading their skills tremendously. At the time, you do not know you are sparring with a champion but keep practicing with them because their wisdom will eventually rub off on you for the better. This is a key choice in your career as a boxer, you need to make sure the people you are sparring with can add value to you. Just like the people in your corner and life, should be able to add value in your life getting you that much closer to winning.

Sparring Lesson

When I was 16 years old, I had a memorable sparring session with a guy much older than me. He was maybe 25 or 26. This guy pulled out all his best techniques. He was getting the best of me in the ring. It seemed like we were in a match rather than a sparring session. His punches caught me off guard, and I was stunned by some of the hits. His trainer paused the sparring session and told me we could stop the session all together because it was getting too rough. His experience clearly did not match my experience at that point, and he was getting me pretty well. Even at 16, I knew the benefit of sparring and chose to continue. Finishing what I started is something my father always made sure I understood. Needless to say, I continued to fight and got a second wind and made the 25-year-old boxer give up. My opponent quit, and I won because I refused to give up.

I had the pleasure of sparring with a guy who came from Colorado. This guy was bigger than me and had a couple pro bouts all won by KO (knockout). When I learned of his record, I knew I had to be at my best. Some people that were around me instantly started talking fear and I had to silence the defeating conversations. We will learn about fear later on in the book. The first round he came out hard and fast. He was aggressive in landing his punches while talking lots of trash. After that round, I had weathered the worst he could possibly give me. In between rounds I thought to myself, "was that the worst he can give me?" When it was time to get back in the ring, I realized I could take more than he could throw, and even give out more. I was good to go. The trash talking stopped and I was in my zone. The last round came, and I hit him with all I had. There was an outpour of punches threw by me, and I never stopped throwing until the bell rang. Moral of the story do not indulge into the hype because one-person's experience is not the same story for you. Your goals will look intimidating at times and sometimes seem like a moving target, but just keep giving it your all and watch yourself strike the target.

Contender's Corner

An unknown person once said: "Amateurs' practice until they get things right. Professionals practice until they cannot get things wrong." Keep practicing and never stop. You never stop learning and developing. That first round was discipline for a great reason: you need discipline in order to keep sparring in life towards those goals to get to those successful wins. The goal is to be undefeated and get as many knockouts as possible.

Think about these questions as we move to the next round.

- When you need help to get ready to conquer a goal, who do you call?

- How has sparring (practicing) been effective in your life?

- What have you asked of your team/supporters specifically to help you with to improve in a certain area?

- Do you feel like you have mastered a skill that will aid you in getting to the next level? If so, what was the skill?

- Thinking about your sparring sessions or route to get

there, would you do anything different? Why or why not?

The next round gets me excited because I would not have gotten where I am now, if I had not had a great team in my corner. Your corner man determines your latitude in life.

Ding, Ding, Ding. Round 3!

Round 3:

Circle

"Who's Your Corner Man"

"The greatest asset, even in this country, is not oil and gas. It's integrity" Everyone is searching for it, asking, 'Who can I do business with that I can trust?"
– George Foreman

You assumed that that last round was going to be easy, right? Trust me, I was once like you. I was so anxious to get in the ring and actually throw punches, but my lack of training schooled me. This is a part of the growing process. Do not give up, there will always be more battles. It is not how you start, but how you finish that truly matters. One thing that is very important in reaching goals is the energy around you, your squad, or your circle. Your circle will determine how far you will go, so pick wisely. Who is your corner man? Who is in your circle? In boxing, a corner man is the coach or teammate assisting the fighter during the length of the match. Their purpose is to get a view point that the boxer does not see in the ring and give suggestions on how to win. This person encourages the boxer to dig deep and keep fighting to get to the ultimate goal. This person is also a soundboard for the boxer with his/her best interest at heart. Now some of you may have to rethink the question. Who is your corner man? Who are you kicking it with? Think about the people that you spend the most time with that might have a direct influence in your life. Are those people rooting for you and offering sound advice? Do they support you mentally and spiritually? Do they work as hard as you? Are they a hindrance or help in your life? Who is your corner man? Your circle probably just got smaller, right? Mine certainly did.

We all start off with a sizeable number of friends growing up and sometimes find out the hard way that we need to cut them off. Have you experienced that one person in your life that always attracts drama and drains your energy? It feels like every time you leave the presence of that person, you feel drained. I can attest to it and I had to assess my circle to weed those people out. As we get older and move towards purpose in our life, our circle can get smaller. My mom always says: "if you want to know where you will be in five years, look around at your circle." I have found this to be a true statement. When the people in your circle are not valuable to where you are going, and you continue to allow them in your space, you can bet you will kiss the canvas, the bottom of the boxing ring.

Do Not Get Clinched

If your corner men are people that don't possess a winning mindset, then you will lose, simply put. Boxer's sometimes have to clinch in order to stay afloat in the ring. Clinching is pegged as a lifesaving technique in boxing. During an intense match when the boxer is trying to restrict the movement of his opponent's arm inside troublesome situations, he is literally fighting to win. On the verge of a knockout or to regain strength for the last rounds of the match, the boxer will lean in and tangle their opponent's arms, so they cannot throw punches. Unproductive corner men are like a clinch, they constantly restrict you from being a champion. Despite all your punches, they restrict your progress, your dreams, your ideas and most importantly you. If you are on the verge of knocking down your goals in life and making some strides, and your corner man stifles it, let them go and never look back.

A great illustration of this is when Joe Frazier and Muhammad Ali fought for the first time on March 8th, 1971. The Fight of the Century was what it was referred to as. This fight displayed great clinching techniques by both champions during the last round of the match. This was the first time two undefeated boxers fought each other for the heavyweight title. Each of these boxers were used to winning and they worked hard. Both boxers were fighting for their lives and during the last round Joe Frazier came out the victor.

Case in point, do not get hemmed up on the rings by a useless corner man. Time is too valuable, and the clock is ticking.

Identifying Your Corner Man

One of my corner men is Bert, he is one of my boxing trainers. Then of course I have my mom and dad and a few other mentors who are just as competitive as myself, they keep me motivated to become my best self, so I can live my best life. My stablemates motivate me by encouraging me and providing me with sound advice. Then I have a few people outside of the boxing ring that are just as supportive and motivating for me as I am for them. The rare times when I am not working out or training for a match, I get to hang out with my friends and my circle is tightly knitted. Not all of them are boxers, but they are all of the same mindset as me and they all have an attitude to win.

Bert, my trainer, makes sure I am always disciplined and staying on top of my physical strength as well as my mental strength. One particular match I had was frustrating me. The first round was filled with unsuccessful punches on my part and that was wearing down my stamina, quickly. I kept trying to land punches on my opponent, serving my best combo punches, but was continuously obstructed. After the first round of me dancing around and trying to land punches, Bert gave me a game plan as to how to beat my challenger as soon as I went back to my corner. My corner man was ready and willing to give motivation and strategy as to how I could get the win. You see, me being in the ring only gave me a certain perspective. Bert had a view that I did not have, and he was able to give advice. The advice would only work if I trusted him and his opinion about my fight. Once the break was over, I got back in the fight and executed just as Bert suggested. Each time I did a stutter step, the guy's feet froze allowing me to step to the right and throw all sorts of punches based on that small adjustment. I was caught up in the moment and was not able to see that. Had he not been there, I would not have been successful. The end of the second round up to the third round went like that, stutter step, then me landing punches and combos. Needless to say, the match was a win for me. Your corner man makes you better.

My father, another corner man in my life, always asked me why I wanted to fight and I my answer was always the same, "because I loved it and wanted to win." He wanted to be certain this was something I was doing for myself and not anyone else. Another quality of an excellent corner man is one who cares about your intentions and does regular checks to see where your head space is. My father also told me that I can be better than him because the Bible says that each generation gets better and better. Now, your friends that are your corner men may not express to you that they want you to better than them, but those people who you look up to or are your parents/family will.

My mother, a corner man in my life also, is always concerned about me during matches. So much so that she cannot stand to watch me fight. She says it is hard to watch me get hit in the ring; her first instinct is to jump in and protect her child, which is an additional quality of a corner man, to protect. My mom laid out sound advice for me as a boxer in order for me to be successful. "Never miss a practice, train hard, NO EXCUSES, take your vitamins, eat well, be disciplined and most importantly, get to know the Lord because you are going to need Him." We all need him. My faith in God is what has kept me and continues to provide strength to me.

The people you choose to stand in your corner must be willing to go the distance during all times of this journey, pick wisely.

Contender's Corner:

Following instructions while in the ring is necessary to being successful. We almost got hit below the belt because that last round required some skills we were not prepared for, but I think we have successfully mastered sparring, and will continue to master certain skills as your career progresses. The people that are offering those instructions and trying to get you through life are significant and matter to your survival rate of the next round. The circle you have around you or the people you seek counsel from will determine the distance you travel on this journey. Pick wisely so you will not have to go through the hassle of getting disqualified for hitting below the belt.

- Think about your core circle, are they preparing you to get to the next level?

- Are they keeping your best interest at heart?

- Are they able to motivate you to keep pushing?

- Do they have a winner's mindset?

- Do they provide perspective?

- Are they able to encourage you to become a better version of you?

- Can they provide sound counsel?

- Are they spiritually equipped to help you fight through challenging times?

If you answered no, to any of these questions, you need to reconsider your circle because the next 9 rounds will require people that are there to see you succeed and are willing to help you get there. Winners have no time to pull dead weight because it slows *us* down and makes *us* lose focus.

Round 4:

Mindset

"You are Who You Think You Are"

"To be a great champion, you must believe you are. If you're not, pretend you are." - Muhammad Ali

You're an amateur boxer! You made it, sounds good right? We have to remember to thank the corner men from the 3rd round that helped us reach this milestone and thank them for their continued support throughout this match. We have a tough road ahead of us to get to the professional level, but we've got this. Awesome thing about this is, I'm an amateur boxer as well so we will be learning from one another and correcting mistakes together. We will serve as each other's corner men. In life, sometimes it is easier when you walk with someone who knows what you are experiencing and can offer some sound advice in those tough times. In this 4th round, we will learn how to focus and to develop a winner's mindset. In order to be a champion you have to have a high level of focus to keep you moving. The tasks at hand will start to show you how prioritizing your obligations are essential to success. Work hard now then play later is another idea we will explore, which is self-explanatory, but sometimes people confuse it and fall short of their duties.

The first thing we talked about as a novice boxer was discipline, so we should now know better. If we keep our thought process positive, we will do well this round. Being a boxer depends 90% on your mentality and 10% on your physical ability. With that being said, I want you to be thinking about how you prepare for a fight. What is your game ritual? Again, I like to refer to mine as the four P's: **Prayer**, **Peace**, **Paint** a Picture, and **Prepare** for the win. This will change from person to person. The way your game ritual looks will not be identical to anyone else's, but the four "P's", the blueprint should. My game rituals are pretty straightforward. I say a prayer for strength and protection. I only think positive thoughts while listening to some of my favorite music. I run through hundreds of possible ways the fight can sway, and then I think of ways to out maneuver my opponent. I find a solution for them all, affirming myself and prepare for the victory.

"For as he thinks in his heart, so *is* he." Proverbs 23:7 [NKJV] The mindset of a person and more importantly how he thinks of himself is what he is, the Bible tells us this perfectly. If you think you are a winner, then you are. This grey mass we have in our skull is powerful and with the right training, you can think of endless things and achieve them. Whatever you can conceive in your mind, you can make it come to pass. If you think you are the greatest, then you are. If you think you will overcome any stumbling blocks, then you will. On the opposite side of that, if you think with defeat you are already defeated before you start the tasks. It is just as important to exercise your brain as it is your body. That comes with saying daily affirmations and guarding what you watch and listen to on a daily basis. Those thoughts can alter your mindset. Certain thoughts will help you focus for your betterment while some thoughts can cause your demise. Since we are on a winning journey, we will think how winners think to stay focused no matter what comes our way. I will not let you get off course, I have been off course and it does not help your goals.

Your new role as an amateur boxer will require you to learn how to embrace struggle and celebrate victory. With the correct mindset you will go far in life, but it all starts with the "winner's mentality."

Rumble in the Jungle

The great Muhammad Ali is an excellent example of how your mindset is important. Ali was claiming to be the greatest boxer well before he was. He knew early on that however you think is so. He was named the greatest Heavyweight boxing Champion of the world. His title spoke for itself, 61 wins, 5 losses, 37 by KO. Muhammad's tactics including boasting on himself and his abilities to his opponents and to anyone who would listen. One of his most memorable fights in history was the "Rumble in the Jungle" or "The Thriller in Manilla." Muhammad Ali was known for talking trash, but it was simply him affirming himself. Ali said things like: *"I am the greatest" "Float like a butterfly, sting like a bee," "I'm so fast that last night I turned off the light switch in my hotel room and was in bed before the room was dark." His claims were cocky to some and confidence to others. Either way your judgment scale tipped, Ali believed in himself. Champions believe in themselves.* Ali admitted that most of those things he said before he knew he was great. His mindset was brilliant.

This is the kind of mindset us amateurs should have, a "can do" attitude by keeping your focus on the prize, no matter what odds are stacked up against you in life. You must pull from all your resources to create a plan for success.

On October 29th, 1974 Ali and Foreman were gloved up to fight in one of the biggest and matches in the 20th century. Foreman was the top contender at the time and held the belt. Ali had already made up in his mind that he was going to take the belt. In 1974, a lot of things were different and to have 60,000 spectators deep in the Congo was a big deal. The televised event would draw 1 billion viewers. 1 billion! That is like having 500,000,000 million YouTube views in 2018 -- mind blowing! Ali was the underdog coming into this match, but with Ali's strong mindset and laser sharp focus, Foreman did not stand a chance against Ali. Ali talked big trash before this match, but he supported all his claims and even introduced a new move called the "Rope-a-Dope" at this match. The "Rope-a-Dope" is when the contender lets the opponent make tireless swings at him in order to wear out the opponent, then the contender executes some devastating maneuvers to win the match. This maneuver helped Ali get the win and knockout George Foreman in the 8th round regardless of all the odds, Ali persevered.

Focus Now Play Later

How focused are you? Time will tell. The road to getting the title belt or crushing your goals will be a direct

29

reflection of how hard you are focused to get there. Many distractions will come your way, trust me. You must be strong enough and smart enough to know what deserves your attention. Before I have a fight, my goal is to focus on the positive things, like winning. I imagine myself winning to help drive all negative thoughts that may try to manifest. I also watch what comes out of my mouth, words have power. Now this is not an easy thing to do, especially if you are just learning this skill. I struggle with it sometimes and I get back up and try again. It is ok to fall, but the key is to get back up with a new approach. Get back up stronger.

I recall a time when my focus was tested. It not only affected me, but my mom more so than me. I was 16 years old and all my mom was trying to do was pay my fees, so I could compete in a fight. Out of nowhere this very irate woman started screaming at my mother and provoking her to fight. At that point, my mom was confused because she had no idea what was going on and of course my mother was not going to fight. This lady had some fight in her and was zeroed in on my mom as the target. She kept trying to launch at my mom, but some men got in between them and broke it up. After the would-be squabble was over, my mom asked me if I still wanted to fight. She felt like my focus was off, but it was far from it. I knew that was a ploy to get my mind uneasy, but all it did was make me more anxious to get into the box and fight. I had worked too hard to let this distraction knock me off my square. Against my mother's better judgement, I went ahead and fought in the tournament. Her logic was that all the commotion and drama would directly affect my match for the worse. Nonetheless, it had the opposite affect and I did excellent in the tournament and took home the gold. My focus never shifted from my goal. After the fight was over, my mother and the woman talked things through and they both realized it was just a misunderstanding. The two of them made peace and laughed about it afterwards. We sometimes think that distractions have the power to hinder our goals but in life we will always have distractions, the key is to not allow them to get in your way and to notice that the way you view them might encourage you to stop moving forward.

After you have completed your goals and you are waiting to tackle the next set you can breathe a little bit, celebrate yourself, then get back on the ground running for the next goals to crush.

When your focus and mindset is on point, then you have already won, the tough part is already achieved.

Contender's Corner

As we discovered in this round, having the right mindset takes you to new levels and makes the difference in the outcome of your goals. If you stay focused on what you came to do, then that is half the battle. Keeping the right people around you and listening and speaking the right words will take you very far in life.

- What does your game ritual look like?
- What are some of your daily affirmations?
- What is your mentality like after a win or a loss?

This next round will show me how responsible you are as a champion. In any direction you go in life, you have to be held accountable for what you say, what you do, who you hang with, and your mentality. This is another great principle to learn early in life. NO EXCUSES.

31

Round 5:

Accountability

"The Blame is On You"

"There is no quit in me." – Larry Holmes

Let us ease into round five. No pressure here. Round four forced us to stretch our thinking in ways we have not done before. That is almost as draining as completing three 2 to 3 hour workouts in one day. I know you think you need rest, but I want you to dig deeper in this round. A little tiredness never hurt anybody, but a little laziness did. Your goals and dreams do not care how you feel physically or even mentally for that matter. If it is in your heart to achieve, you will always give it your best shot at a slower pace. Some pace is more honorable than no pace.

Round five is all about accountability. You have to be responsible for yourself at all times, especially when you do not want to be. Yes, I said it! Newsflash: sometimes you do not want to be responsible! I would not be a great trainer if I did not tell you that days will come when you will *"not feel like it,"* but those are the days you work harder and push through. Especially since we have already established that our goals do not care how we feel. But that is where our accountability steps in and motivates us to fight through them. In life, we will not always have a check and balance system, so you have to check and balance yourselves. Having an accountability partner can be useful to some people. An accountability partner is a person who coaches you through a commitment you agreed to keep. Just that simple. Sort of like a conscious with the poor reasoning on the left shoulder and the logical reasoning on the right. A checks and balance partner. Now your accountability partner can be someone within your circle or one of your corner men. Keep in mind, the accountability partner needs to be someone who reciprocates the same, if not, similar work ethic as you. They must have some solid goals they are working towards in order to help you stay focused on yours. In boxing it can be your sparring partner, as you all share similar goals. In other areas, it can be a classmate, a peer, a business partner, or someone who is like minded and has similar goals. If you do not have one, think about who that person can be in your life and what that would look like.

On the other hand, we have all encountered those people who always has an excuse as to why they did not accomplish their goals or go after their dreams. **DO NOT BE THAT PERSON**. This would not be a great example of an accountability partner. They sound like a scratched record on one of those old school record players, with a bent needle. Irritating and unproductive. It would be the equivalent of sparring with a toddler, useless and a waste of time. Investing your time wisely more than half of the time is a good indicator that you are responsible and are on the road to becoming accountable for the road you travel down in your life.

The Onus Falls on Us

Accountability is significant because as a boxer, which is unlike any other sport, the onus falls on you alone. In organized sports there is a structured team and game plan. Players are held accountable by a team of coaches and other teammates. The "team" member plays an intricate part of the team and without each player doing their part the team will suffer. A boxer does not have the luxury of a "team" in the ring. Boxers have to mostly hold themselves accountable for the win or loss in a match. Traveling towards your dreams is sometimes a lonely road, the responsibility falls on you; a group of people are not playing intricate parts of a team to achieve a common goal. Do not misunderstand me, you do have motivators and people coaching along the way, but if the plan does not work, it is your own responsibility.

Boxers do have to do countless things on their own. One in particular is financing their own dream for several years without pay. This is a tall order for an athlete, but in order to be successful it has to be done. Accountability goes hand and hand with discipline. Like I stated earlier it is easier to walk through life with people who understand your working conditions, but sometimes that is not always the case. Accountability sets the fighters apart in life and in the boxing ring. Each boxer must push themselves to the absolute limit, to do things they might not necessarily want to as I mentioned earlier.

A younger fighter does not have it easy because many things will catch their attention and challenge their attentiveness to focus. If you are not accountable to yourself, you will pay for it in the ring. There have been a couple of times where I have to push myself to get up and work through the soreness of my body after a five-day competition. Although I have a high tolerance to pain like my father, ignoring the soreness or uncomfortableness is sometimes necessary to complete my goals. When I am focused on the win, somehow the pain isn't an obstacle. This type of thinking is what it takes to be the best. And you will develop this thinking at some point too. The most important part is that you get back to work. Accountability is something we continue to work on and work through. It is a lifelong feat. I'm a 20-year-old man, who is often tempted by the same things the average 20-year-old man encounters daily. As I get older, I embrace and am reminded that I am ultimately responsible for my choices. You will find this to be true in your own life, but continue to work through it, even when you fall short.

Boxing, they say is a thinking man's sport. I think that trying to hold oneself accountable without the support of family and trainers can be rough for boxers and we can easily lose focus with the various distractions. At the end of the day it's all about who wants it badly enough and who will endure until they decide to turn pro. Boxing is a sport that does not pay off for many years and some boxers can lose the hunger for it within that time. An amateur boxer can box for years for free, just as I have boxed since I was 12. No pay. No names in lights. Just a thirst to want to become the best boxer I can.

Amateurs fight everybody and anybody, some of them have over 100 fights under their belts. They are in wars way before they can go pro. Financing a good boxing program can be expensive. They have to pay for the boxing gear, coaches, travel, and fees to get into fights. If one does not have the finances, they can't continue boxing not unless they get a sponsor.

Accountability has to be taught, practiced and repeated. On the road to your goals you will be tested, and sometimes you will fail the test and other times you will ace it with flying colors. Main thing to remember is to be consistent in your discipline and the accountability will follow.

Contender's Corner

Accountability prepares one to be a leader for themselves, it prepares them to take on any challenge that life presents to them. When you become accustomed to doing necessary things in life to win, accountability is second nature. Your mindset has to be strong and keep growing to be stronger every day because new challenges will test you when you climb to higher levels. I can tell you that you need to be disciplined until I am blue in the face, but until you are defeated from not being prepared or disciplined, in the ring or in life, you will not understand accountability to the fullest.

Let's reflect on the below questions.

- Envision your ideal accountability partner. What qualities will they need to possess? What abilities and type of attitude will they need to have? Describe them in detail.

- Have you ever done anything in the past, that you did not hold yourself accountable for and because of it, you suffered or others? Explain the situation.

- What would you have done differently?

It is now time to pick up the pace. Your fight will intensify from here until the end, just as life does when you are on a path to greatness. You are attaining all these nuggets because you have to take what you learned and apply them in round 12.

Round 6:

Pressure

"Fighters find it hard to give up doing what they do best – fighting for a living." – Evander Holyfield

Whoa! Your opponent came out swinging like Mike and you barely landed a punch. You have a busted lip, but that is ok, you kept fighting and I like that. You are going to be my best protege yet and all of our goals in life will be crushed. We are now halfway to the title fight.

Insurmountable pressure is to be expected when in the boxing ring. The goal in mind of each boxer is to win, but there is only one winner. One boxer out works or out smarts the other to determine a winner. Which one will you decide to become on your journey in life when you are faced with overwhelming pressure? Remember this: there are two types of pressure, the pressure that bust pipes and the pressure that produces diamonds. Pressure is a great influencer to have during your road to the championship because pressure is how diamonds are formed. You start out as a lump of coal but end up a precious stone if you persevere and push through. We are halfway complete, and I

40

believe you can make it to the championship round and win. A little pressure never hurt a champion.

Boxing has taught me numerous things and one is to always be ready for anything. When the pressure mounts, my anxiety levels usually follow. This is when my unshakable faith ignites; allowing me to be able to sit in it and not be affected. My faith is what carries me through making the route look easy on the outside. Do not let the pressure of situations veer you off course of your ultimate goal to win. I have witnessed how pressure will get the best of some great athletes and cause them to fold and not perform to their ultimate level of success.

On September 18th, 1999, Oscar De La Hoya and Felix Trinidad had a boxing match called, "The Fight of the Millennium". The name of the fight was pressure in itself. It was the last fight of the year 1999 and would be a memorable one for all involved. Who would want to lose a fight of this magnitude? The answer is quite simple, neither boxer, but the problem is that there can only be one winner. This fight was a big deal and the surge in betting was more than boxing had seen in a great while. Spectators were excited to witness this match, but in the end, the fight did not nearly live up to its expectations. Oscar De La Hoya was defeated by Felix Trinidad. Sometimes pressure will get the best of you in life and you will get caught up in the moment and fold to all the pressure being applied. I am almost certain De La Hoya went to the match with the expectation of winning, but Trinidad rose above the pressure and won.

Mike Who?

By the time I was 15 years old, my game, my discipline, and my passion for the sport of boxing had become more apparent. Boxing was my happy place. I excelled in it. During this one particular match, I was due to fight and I was ready. My aunts, friends, and other family were there to support me. It was a pretty huge deal, and I tried not to think about it too much. Upon getting ready for the fight in the back, I performed my game rituals and was ready to attack. Once I got to the ring there were cameras everywhere and the crowd was so hyped. The energy of the crowd let me know I had to turn up. The adrenaline pumping through my veins were enough for two eager boxers. It was show time. The bright lights and cheers in the room provided encouragement for my machine to perform at its best. This was the ideal atmosphere for a great fight to be held. I looked in my opponent's eyes and was ready to do what champs do, win. Before the bell sounded, the announcer said, "we have two heavyweight champions of the world in the building he said, "Mike Tyson and Evander Holyfield," The spectators went wild creating a level of pressure I had never experienced at that point in my life. I was full of emotion and did not know how to feel. All I could think was, "I cannot be beat up in front of my father, my friends, family, this enormous crowd, and now Mike Tyson." I had already known of Mike, but he had never come to any of my matches. There is one thing to know greatness, but it's another thing to be in the same profession as them, and know they have to watch you perform. The only thing I could think about was not messing up in front of Mike Tyson and my father.

Within a few seconds I had to let all of this information process. The loads of energy I had right before this seemed to drain fast like an iPhone on 2%, with all my apps open. All these thoughts are going through my mind, but I knew I still had to go out there and do my job and win. I'm a champion and champions never quit, even under pressure. Once that bell rang and the first punch was thrown, I was ready to rumble. I was not going to let my opponent win, so I outboxed him.

I commenced to throwing my punches, using my best combos and working my opponent. During the fight my shoelace came untied, this rarely happens in my fights. Mike Tyson started yelling, "Evan you gotta f&@$ him up. You gotta punch like this." Imagine taking directives from two heavyweight champions of the world, at the same time. Talk about tension. Then Mike kept coming up to the ring while I was in the corner and in the ring saying, "Evan you better f%$@ him up, you better f$%@ him up!" Mike was being Mike and his being there showed me that I could fight under any sort of pressure, but more pressure was yet to come.

I'm Holyfield, Evan Holyfield!

Being the son of a celebrity is one feat in itself. But following in the same footsteps as your dad is a whole other level. There is immense pressure on me to be "like" my father from the world, when I am striving to be like me, Evan. Many times, when I am announced at matches the announcer will say, "Evander Holyfield's son, Evan Holyfield, is competing against whomever". Automatically I am looked at as my father and so the comparing eye starts. "He is nothing like his dad," was a statement made by one announcer during a fight. Thank God I did not get frustrated and thrown off my square because of the comments. Of course, I am not like my dad, I'm EVAN! These people got the pleasure seeing my father as a professional boxer and at the height of his career. But they do not keep that in mind when they are comparing me, at my amateur level, to my father's pro level. They certainly did not see my father during his amateur years, so what they see is a limited snapshot of his entire career. I just get in the ring and put up my best fight as Evan Holyfield.

I have even had guys get hyped up because they are fighting me. In their minds, they are fighting Evander Holyfield, "The Real Deal Holyfield". When they hear my last name, their mind takes them somewhere and they equate "Holyfield" to Evander and not Evan. After some of my fights my friends and family could hear my opponents flexing, saying, "I just fought a heavyweight champion of the world, Holyfield," when in actuality, they fought me, Evan, the amateur. This creates pressure because now I have to work twice as hard to prove them wrong.

The general consensus is that life is handed to me on a silver platter, when that is far from the truth. I have had to work extra hard to prove that I am worthy to be here, and I must pave my own path to success. My father does not train me or has ever trained me, except for my very first fight. I am actually in the gym putting in the work to earn my stripes in this sport. Nothing is given to you, you must earn it and the same rules apply to me. It would not feel like I earned it if everything was given to me. My parents raised me to set goals for myself to achieve success and be the best version of myself. I did not get bumped up in ranks because of my name or my father. Most fights I won or lost fair and square and there are a couple I still question.

Contender's Corner:

To perform at your optimum level, you need to be put under some type of pressure to see if you will sink or swim. The speed at which the punches have been thrown during this round made me think you were not able to maintain. I saw you staggering, but through all the stress you made it out. I know we are on our way to a victory. Life will apply enormous pressures, dividing the strong from the weak. We just learned in the last round that your mindset has to be right or else you will suffer. All the skills we have been through so far have prepared you well for this round. When it was time to persevere, you came through and did not disappoint.

In life you will be compared to people but don't accept it as your vision for yourself. Teachers will compare you to other students, friends will compare you to other friends and maybe you compare yourself to others on social media. Sometimes parents will compare you to your brothers and sisters thinking that it will make you improve upon your weaknesses. This can be draining especially if you feel like you cannot live up to the demands. I am constantly compared to my father, but I just go in the ring and show them Evan. The bottom line is that you can't stop people from comparing you against other's, but you can control how you think about it and how you respond. Don't ever allow what others say about you stop you from achieving your goals.

Complete the questions below before you move to the next round.

- Think of a time in your life where you were faced with great pressure to complete a challenge, what was the challenge and how did you perform?

- Did you learn from the pressure? What was the valuable lesson you learned?

- Have you ever experienced having to do something that you were a beginner at while others with more experience looked on? If so, how did it make you feel?

- How did it further prepare you to reach any goals you may have?

- Have you ever had to be compared to an older sibling or family member in regards to your performance or reaching goals? If so, how did it make you feel?

Round 7:

Adversity

"Fighting Through Adversity"

"A true champion will fight through anything."
– Floyd Mayweather

You aren't tired, are you? I know you still have more fight in you. Champions fight through anything and know how to overcome adversity. This round will introduce some new punch combinations that you have yet to see, but I need you to keep fighting. In essence, there are only six punches you can actually throw, but you know that by now since you are now on your professional fighter journey. Your novice level ended a while back and presented you with some hits that you were not familiar with, and you conquered it nonetheless. A few mistakes were made, but you made the necessary corrections to learn from them. The amateur road was like a walk in the park, you went hard and gave your all. Now that you are a professional, I need you to understand that you can come up with thousands of punch combinations, you can get creative as you need to win the title belt. This fight is like whatever you are working towards in your personal life, each round you got better, and each combination punch you created was a route to get you closer to the win of your goal in life. This type of fight is only for the strong physically, mentally and spiritually.

Don't lose the faith. The last thing I want to do is evoke fear inside of you. I want you to tap into your arsenal, so you can be prepared for any hit that may come at you. When you are traveling through this life, towards your goals, there will be many setbacks or left hooks, the unexpected ones, and you have to know how to take a hit, avoid a hit and keep swinging. Life will sometimes punch you unexpectedly, which will oftentimes flicker your likes or knock you through the ropes. Just remember, if you fall through the ropes, you have a 20 count to get back up on your feet and get back in the ring. No one can assist you, this has to be on your own merit or else the referee will call it a knockout. Do not let your goals knock you out, I want you to get back up every single time.

This round requires your undivided attention because by the end of this round, you will need to pull from your arsenal and push through no matter what. I am counting on you. I just shared with you how to not let pressure get the best of you when it is applied. In life, there will be unexpected jabs or hurdles that will present themselves and it's all about your mindset and preparation that produces your comeback. All the work you put in behind closed doors will have prepared you for what is to come. Trust me, the way you have trained and sacrificed behind closed doors has equipped you with more than you think. You may be wondering, do I get apprehensive at the unknown, of course, but my winning mindset takes over all the time. I can knockout obstacles no matter how long it takes me. You can too. Us champions fight through anything!

One, Two, Bite!

June 28th, 1997, twenty-one years ago, Mike Tyson and Evander Holyfield, my father, fought at the MGM Grand in Las Vegas. This fight was called the "Sound and the Fury". They were fighting for the heavyweight championship belt. Stakes were high because they had fought seven months earlier and my father had knocked down Tyson in the 11th round and took the championship belt. According to Tyson, he already had rage in him from the last loss to my dad and was ready to snatch the title by any means necessary. The fight ensued and Holyfield [my dad] was accused of headbutting, which my dad says isn't true. Mike bit a chunk of flesh from my dad's ear and a timeout was called. There was blood and my father just kept fighting like the champion he is. My dad is a fighter and true champion. He always taught me to never run from a setback, but to get ready for your comeback instead. Just as my father had instilled in me my entire life, overcoming adversity was being displayed that night, and to the entire world of viewers. And that's what I do, I apply that example to my own life when I face adversity.

The bell rang, and the fight was back on. The round started and shortly into the fight, Tyson bit another of chunk of flesh from my dad's ear and the bout was stopped for good and Tyson was disqualified in the third round. My dad retained the heavyweight belt. That story let me know that true champions fight through anything and you can too. This infamous fight between two great champions showed the hunger, emotion and passion for attaining their goals.

The unexpected ear bite did not stop my dad from putting

his best effort forward to continue fighting. No matter what sneaks up on you, you must keep moving, no matter how it hurts or how embarrassing it may be, just keep going.

Speak on It

When I was younger, I had to work extra hard to prove myself because of my small size. That could've been a jab to my self-esteem, but I kept it moving to fight through it. I was called the skinny kid with a big head, which was true, but people loved to remind me of what I saw each day like they too did not experience an awkward stage. Only thing was, my awkward stage lasted longer than I wanted it to, but those were the cards I was dealt, and I played my hand. I learned how to work with what I had to continue to move to greatness. Sometimes in life, when things get tough, we need to develop the great skills we have and be good at it. That is exactly what I did. I was excellent at quite a few things. Had I believed the opinion of others I would have quit long ago. My dad constantly shared his childhood stories with me and how he handled them and came out a winner. I knew my size was temporary. Once you get over what people's perception is of you, you can do anything, and you will not quit, no matter what. Besides, they are entitled to feel how they want. You are better than what other people think of you.

My mother always encouraged me to wait for my time to come. When things got complicated and I even looked like I wanted to stay down for the count, my mother would never let me quit. She always spoke life and encouraged me to stick with it and assured me that I would improve. It is important that your corner men are in tune with you and your needs. Sometimes your cornermen know exactly what you need before you even realize it or mention it to them. Starting something and not finishing the task or goal is not the characteristic of a true champion. Your hype man will go the extra mile to root for you, inspire you, encourage and provide whatever you need to accomplish that goal of winning. No matter if I got playing time during practice or games, my mom made me suit up and go to every game and practice just like my dad did when he was growing up. That is fighting through adversity at its finest. Keep throwing those combos and muddle through. Training myself mentally to find the positive in every situation helped me during those tough times.

When I was younger, I struggled with my speech due to chronic ear infections, so the first few years of my life everything sounded like I was underwater. To combat this, one of the things my mother insisted on me doing was communicating for myself even if I wasn't understood. I was being groomed to deal with adversity early on. According to my mother I was delayed in my speech and most people could not understand me, so I rarely spoke. I know what it feels like to be teased or treated inferior by both adults and kids; however, my close friends were patient and never made me feel different. There again were those corner men in my life at a young age. I had been jabbing and weaving and not even knowing it. Sometimes that is what happens, especially if you feel like you are not getting anywhere, but you keep moving around in that ring and making it count.

Speech therapy consumed a lot of my time from the age of 4 to 8 years of old. Every day after school my mom would drive me to the speech therapist and then transport me to my after-school activities. One day my mother ran into some hurdles with the insurance company because they said I made a 70% improvement and they could no longer allow my mother to make appointments. Not pleased with the discussions of the insurance company, my mother fussed with them telling them that I was still having difficulty speaking clearly. They stood firm with the 70% and said that they would not continue to cover speech therapy. Other people's opinions will sometimes try to convince you that you cannot go any further and that you should be content with what you have and that the next level is too much for you and even too much of a hassle to try to reach. This is when that arsenal of different punch combos come in handy. During this time, I also suffered chronic ear infections which kept me in the emergency room weekly. My ears would drain of infections, I would have high temperatures which required immediate medical assistance. Nonetheless, I kept fighting through to defeat this thing.

My mother told me that she learned speech therapy techniques by watching how the speech pathologist worked with me, so she decided to work with me every day to get my speech to 100%. She would not accept what the insurance company told her. Champions are not satisfied at 70% when 100% is the goal. My mother has a champion spirit as well. Every day we'd practice until she thought I had mastered sounds and letters. That is what you must do; keep working toward your goals until you have mastered them, kinda like sparring. Do not settle for mediocre results because you will start to settle in other areas of life. I have to admit, my mom was tough, but her techniques worked and made me grind harder for the rewards.

Mom would take me to a fast food drive thru after school

often, so I could put to use the new skills I was learning. Kids love fast food burgers and fries and I was no different. The deal was, if the drive thru worker could understand me when I ordered my food, then I would get my meal. This may seem trivial, but to me it was an obstacle that I had to overcome. In my head, I was coaching myself, "Ok Evan time to dig deep in that bag of punches and pull out that best combo to knock it out of the park". I dug deep and yelled my order in the microphone with confidence, and to my dismay the worker did not understand me, so mom drove away. Just like that. Hamburger and french fries were out of reach. As a kid, I was crushed, especially at that young age. All I could think was, why did my mom not take over and order my food? In hindsight, I absolutely understand why. She was teaching me to apply what I knew to get what I wanted, despite what others thought I could achieve. I went back to the drawing board and pulled out another strategy or combo punch to knockout this issue. Well, for three days, the worker could not understand me, and my mother drove away just like she did on day one. Each strategy I tried did not succeed. She told me that I cried, but she was sadder than I was. On the fourth day I was determined to get my kiddie meal and I finally said all of the words clear enough for the worker to understand and that was the last day I had a speech impediment. I had finally figured it out and knew what punches to string together to get the job done. When you are working towards mastering some skill or goal, you will not get it on the first time, but keep working towards it and reward yourself when you master it.

Whew! This round was tough, and I am glad it is over. We had to fight through a lot, but guess what, you did that! I see the champion rising up in you.

Contender's Corner

When the world feels like it is coming down on you through embarrassment or hurt, and you question rather to continue or not, remember that quitting is the last thing you want to do. Fighting through adversity builds character and fearlessness. Giving up is the equivalent of saying you are not good enough to keep fighting for your dreams or goals. You are worthy and are capable of doing so. Where is your integrity? True winners are filled with integrity, which we will talk about in round 8. The saying, winners never quit and quitters never win is a true statement, especially when they are faced with tumultuous times. Best believe the times will get arduous, but you will be well equipped to run the course.

Think about these questions as we move to the next round.

- Think of a time when you had to fight through something you did not think was possible. What did you do the first time? Second time?
- What could you have done better to make overcoming easier?
- What have you learned in this round that will better prepare you for the next obstacle to emerge in your life?

Ok champs, we have now made it to round 8!

Round 7 - Adversity

Round 8:

Integrity

"Responding When No One is Watching"

"Doing the right thing, even when no one is watching." – Unknown

To have integrity means you do the right thing even when no one is watching. It is like finding some money and giving it back to its rightful owner. Everyone gives you slack about it, but you stick to your sound decision. That is integrity. We all have been tested, sometimes without us even realizing it. A true winner will always try to do the right thing. In a few instances, we have all fallen short of making the right choices, quickly get up, take responsibility and learn from it to grow stronger. Being a youth, we are faced with many challenges that will test what we know is right. This is when those great corner people are there to help you when you could veer off course and help hold you accountable.

Round seven showed us how we have to fight through adversity. Fighting through adversity definitely takes some restraint because it is easy to make the wrong decision and lose focus. It takes courage to make the right decisions. My parents always tell me: *people are gonna always size me up for some reason or another.* There is no rhyme or reason as to why, they just do. So, they encourage me to be myself and do me. I am reminded by my parents and my corner men that I am a work in progress. I am going to make mistakes, but the key is to learn from them and do better next time. My mom and dad are pretty transparent, and they remind me of their own mistakes which helps me to know that we're all a work in progress striving to do better and be better.

There are three things I try to do and still work at that I have learned along my journey.

3 Ways to Keep it Real

1.   Keep it 100
Just be yourself. Don't worry about what nobody else thinks or has to say. Do what you feel is right and stick to it.

2.   Control Your Anger

It is easier to get in the ring and be mad, but it is difficult to control your anger when every muscle in your body is tense and you want to pounce. You still must maintain a certain demeanor because boxing is 90% mental. If I can control my anger, my actions can't be tried, and I will make the best move.

3.   Watch Your Words

My dad always encourages me to watch my words. He says they have power and they manifest! This is why I talked about watching what you listen to and say. Junk talk will certainly be a detriment to your body like eating too much junk food when you are training. Always speak life, meaning always speak positive words over your life. And don't listen to others speak negativity over your life.

Showing Up

My father is a great example of showing me what keeping your word means. He showed me more through his actions than anything he could have ever said about being a man of your word.

My father encouraged me to become active in my community by introducing me to boxing leagues, such as the Police Athletic League. It is there that I was able to participate in charity events by boxing to raise money for the police and other community ventures they were a part of. My family has served meals to children in the hospital on holidays and I've fought in several charity events to raise money for children. One thing that my father taught me was to always keep your commitments, even when personal issues arise.

We have all faced hard times within our personal lives and my family is no stranger to it as well. When my dad was forced out of his home, it was a trying time as you can imagine. Outside of the ring, we face stressful times, but it is all in how you respond to them. The very next day after my dad's foreclosure on his home, I participated in a boxing clinic with him at a Boys and Girls club event downtown Atlanta. In that moment, I saw the magnitude of his character. His decision to keep moving despite his situation was the honorable thing to do. Even during hard, difficult times, my dad still kept his word and attended the event to give back to the community. The champ, my dad, showed me how to not allow situations to deter you from doing good for others. I learned to control my emotions and push forward. Feeling sorry for yourself makes the situation seem larger than it actually is. At that point you should think about all the reasons you are grateful. When you are faced with obstacles outside of the ring, whatever you do, maintain your stance on doing what you know is the right thing   to   do.

Contender's Corner:

Being true to yourself will take you far. Keep taking those opportunities to do the right things. Trust me, it is much easier than it sounds, but the champion you are becoming, I have no doubt will be practicing these same principles.

Reflect on the questions below as we move towards the last round.

- Explain a time when you have been faced with a decision and it challenged you at being 100. How did you handle it?

- What could you have done differently or the same?

- How will you apply the 3 principles to keeping it 100 in your life?

Alright champ let's secure the bag in these next rounds.

Let's eat!

Round 9:

Heart

"Champions Never Show Fear"

"This is the game. We win some, we lose some, but I will never shy away from a challenge. - Connor McGregor

Listen – keeping it 100 is essential to a champion but it is not a walk in the park. We are faced with so many challenging things that present us with either taking the easy route or taking the road less travelled. Not you! You have taken the advice that I learned from my cornermen and my dad and used it to get through that round. I can almost guarantee that people were watching you knock out those goals, take those jabs, and uppercut the challenges all while staying true to yourself. It is commendable. Round 9 is not for the weak. In the boxing ring, it is not wise to show your opponent fear, even if you are afraid. Champions are afraid occasionally, but they have learned to fight through it. A true winner can have storms going on inside of them, but the exterior will only present willingness. It's called choosing to ignore the symptoms of fear, failure, defeat, doubt and what the situation looks like.

Fighting scared is never recommended but if you feel it you

must ignore it and keep moving forward. I would rather you continue in a match shaking in your boots, but not showing it than giving up and not even trying. Once you grow you start to train your mind to work harder than those instances; which will be lessened. Some of your dreams are so big that they can scare you, but you know in the back of your mind that they can be accomplished, so you continue to pursue them while putting your best foot forward. After a while, it gets easier and you take more jabs, then you get fancy with the footwork, then you go in for the left hook and smash your goals. Keep this winner's mentality -- you will need it this round! You may have butterflies, but it doesn't mean you are afraid. If you don't do what you are supposed to do then you are afraid. Anytime something makes you not do what you are supposed to do it means you are afraid. You can make mistakes but as long as you show up you are a winner. When you don't show up you are making excuses.

My dad, Evander Holyfield, has spoken to me about not showing any type of emotion, fatigue or pain in the ring. We have had in depth conversations. He said, "Son, once you show people that you are afraid, upset or hurt you give them every reason to have an upper hand." So many of us wear our emotions on our sleeves and we also make decisions based upon how we feel. We will react instead of responding which can spoil the message we want to convey or the desired outcome. Showing emotions and not remaining calm in adverse situations clouds our thinking. In the ring, sometimes all you have is your fearlessness. When you are going after your goals, sometimes all you have is your fearlessness or willingness to do it.

Let's do an exercise, yes, I know we are in the middle of a match, but for you to get this, we must take a break and get this in. Get in the ring or wherever you are and punch at the air or punching bag for three minutes straight, rest 30 seconds and do it two more times until you have totaled nine minutes. Do not worry I will wait. Keep going. I can see you slowing down. I see a grimace and it looks like pain. CHANGE THAT face. Keep the same pace and intensity you had when you started. Let's go. You've got it! Get mad! Get focused in on your path. Now stop. How do you feel? You see how fighting through adversity, fear, stress, fatigue without showing it makes a difference? This is a skill that you will need to practice daily, you must build this. This is nothing you will develop overnight, but in time you will. Your opponent was unaware of anything that you were thinking, and you displayed a champion spirit!

Fear Is Not a Factor

There was a great example of being fearless displayed in a recent fight by two professional athletes. Both on the opposite spectrum of the sport and both tremendously skilled at what they do. Super welterweight champion, Floyd Mayweather and UFC champion, Connor McGregor fought in Las Vegas, Nevada on August 26th, 2017. What makes this fight so iconic is that McGregor is not a boxer but was fearless enough to want to take on the undefeated, Mayweather. This fight was coined, "The Money Fight" because each fighter would take home more than $100,000,000. Mayweather reportedly took home $300,000,000, hence the money fight. This match not only had the murmurs surrounding it about the large amount of money to be earned, but the fact that McGregor was not a traditional boxer was kicking up more dust than Mayweather. McGregor danced around trying to intimidate and knock Mayweather off his square, but when the bell rang, Mayweather would prove to be the champion of the world.

We can safely say that McGregor showed us some heart and fearlessness and because of this he is still considered a champion.

Showing Your Fears Can Hinder You

Young people, I come to be 100% real with you. That is how barriers are knocked out. I am no different than you. We are all striving to become the best version of ourselves, and that means talking about some things that will help someone else grow on their journey.

In amateur boxing, you fight everybody and anybody, quite naturally you have to be prepared for the worst-case scenario. My dad always says "you have to stay ready, so you don't have to get ready", this is what a true champion does because he knows that preparation is a major key to winning. My mother was always concerned about the age and depth of experience in amateur boxing. She often voiced her opinion of how it was not a fair fight. As we know, life is not fair, but you still have to be prepared to take some tough blows and get up and be willing to do it again. Her unfairness argument for amateur boxing was: an amateur boxer could potentially fight another amateur boxer that has fought 100 fights to another fighter who has only fought 10. Once a novice boxer completed his 10th match, he is an open amateur. Just like that no warning, no grandiose entrance, you are now open to fight literally anyone. That means ANYONE! They call them open fights. Then she goes on to say it's like middle school competing in organized sports against high school students or even high school students competing against college level students. In each one of those examples, both groups have more experience and knowledge and could easily defeat the young team. But in amateur boxing that is not a factor, the boxer still has to fight. Remember we have to be ready for anything. If you stay in your boxing stance, you'll never have to get ready. However, there is definitely a downpour of unexpected punches to come.

I recall one open fight, I was just 15 years old. This was probably my only most unexpected fight I can remember. The guy standing across from me in the ring was 18 or19 years old. All I could think about was how many fights he had and his vast experience compared to my 10 or so fights. I created a scenario all in a matter of seconds. Many people came to me and shared his stats and age. In my mind, he was a grown man and I was just 15. I have to fight this "adult" was all I could think about. Seemed like I was going to be in for a long night.

The short three-minute rounds seemed like a 24-hour day. I was almost defeated before I got in the ring because I let my mind and other's size up this guy before I stepped foot in the ring. My opponent could've had some reservations too, but I never got a glimpse of them. We now know that going into the ring with any inkling of doubt may delay your chances of winning in life. That is why mindset is always important, as we talked about in round 5. I may as well had taken off my gloves and set them to the side because my fight could've been lost before I stepped in the ring. He had a beard which made him look much older to me. Basically, my imagination got me distracted.

Later, my dad shared with me a time when he faced the

same challenge. He had to fight a guy named Cecil Collins three times when he was just an amateur like myself. It took him three different times to overcome his fear and finally win. My dad told me that he even put rocks in his shorts so that he didn't have to make weight to fight the guy. He went home and pretended his stomach was hurting to avoid fighting this guy. My dad's mom knew what was going on, so she made him go back and fight the guy. She told him that once he won, he could quit. Well, my dad fought the guy a third time and finally won. Sometimes we will have to face our fears several times before we overcome them. Sometimes, people in our corner will encourage us to keep trying. I am grateful that my dad shared this story with me because I now understand that champions don't always start off champions. Champions overcome many things before they become true champions.

I learned a valuable lesson that day: never size up your opponents or goals. Had I not imagined the worse, I would've knocked the guy out in the first round instead of going three rounds. Learn from my dad's story as well as mine as you are moving through these rounds. Even if you are afraid, keep pushing towards that goal, do it scared. Once you get on the other side of fear, you find that there was not too much to be hesitant about in the first place.

Contender's Corner:

Mindset ready. Check! Fearless ready. Check! This is going to be a gratifying experience. Maybe not at first, but you will appreciate this journey once you look back over your progress. You are transforming in front of my eyes. You have taken what I have shared with you and applied it to your own life. Continue to use what I have learned from my father and my cornermen, while remembering the fearlessness it takes to become the title holder for the championship. You will be undefeated, it's inevitable.

Think about the questions below as you look at your personal encounters with fear.

- Think of a time when you were afraid, and you kept moving towards your goal. What was the goal and what was the outcome?

- Name someone in your life that is fearless and why.

 Your hard work is paying off, I see a professional boxer on the horizons.

Round 10, we are in it to win it!

Round 10:

Winning & Losing

"Make the Best of It All"

*"The fight is won or lost far away from witnesses –
behind the lines, in the gym, and out there on the
road, long before I dance under those lights."* –
Muhammad Ali

My dad was hanging out in the boxing gym just shooting the breeze with everybody, and we started talking about Mike Tyson. My dad said, "A lot of times when you get winded and tired, this is where people's thinking starts changing." "They start thinking about how tired they are. When you are in shape you are not thinking about being tired."" If you get hurt, something is gonna change." "*Like when Mike Tyson says everybody got a plan till, they get hit in the face.*" "*If you feel that you are hurting then things start to change.*" When my dad got hit, he always got a little bit more aggressive. He says, you have to match what happens to you in the ring. Your opponent begins to change their mind about hitting you back because they felt the sting of your punches. "Whoever gets tired first is the one who will most likely lose." So, the key to winning in anything is preparation. Always practice as much as you can.

So, with all of that said, fear cannot be a factor for us. Whenever a giant is presented to us champions, we make adjustments to knock it out or find a way around it. You cannot keep your focus on winning if you are afraid. Make the giant uncomfortable by getting just as aggressive as he or she is. Be willing to make adjustments. I know things seemed a bit harder when we first started, but you were a novice then, and since you have won a few fights you are equipped with all of the tools you need in boxing or your life. Champions never stop learning. Even if they win or lose a match; an opportunity to sharpen your skills will arise. What will you do if you lose at something you were aiming towards at life? Do you quit? Do you fold? You only lose if you don't try. No, you adjust, and you shake it off and get back in the ring. Losses are lessons, when you have the right mindset. Like I said, until now, you have powered through each round bringing out the beast in you. You struggled a moment, and I thought I was going to have to call the round, but you dug deep, persevered. This round may not be as easy you for, but it is definitely worth it. In life, we have to do things that we do not want to do, but the benefits far outweigh being uncomfortable for a limited amount of time. There is much growth in being uncomfortable. Just remember everything I have told you thus far, apply where necessary. Tighten up those gloves it's time to rumble.

Its effortless to bounce back and let go when you are winning. For example, acing those tests in school, being popular among all your peers, or receiving high praises for the excellent strides you are making on your job. It is seamless to have your chest sticking out. Almost like bragging. Victories last, but only a short time and you always need to be thinking about how you can improve. If you find yourself on the losing side of things, you should always review the fights, measure yourself, reflect on what went wrong, and try not to focus on the negative. Perhaps you could have done more or performed better but promise yourself that you will not dwell on all of the negatives. Instead focus on how far you have come and how far you have to travel down your road. Negative thoughts only lead you down a path of destruction. For example, "why did I fail this test with a 60%, I was almost there," "why am I not the popular one now, I have just as much, if not more than those other kids" and "this job sucks I only made one error and now I'm being written up." Each fight or setback in life you face, your mindset should always get back to winning, no matter that previous outcome. Losing can make you better at whatever you are striving for, only if you take the loss as a tool. This is how you gain confidence if you focus on improvement instead of defeat in *all* situations. The more fights you have the more ways you will be able to think about more ways to win, especially after losing. Remember: *"A setback only paves the way for a comeback."* – Evander Holyfield

"No Mas"

December 7th, 1989, Sugar Ray Leonard triumphs over a mediocre performance by Roberto Duran in a unanimous 12-round decision. This would be the 3rd and final time these two are in the ring together. The last two matches left both of the boxers tied and Duran wanted to claim back his title, but ultimately Leonard came out the victor. Expectations were high and of course there could only be one winner, but this unanimous decision proved that neither wanted to lose. One out worked the other and all the judges agreed. The Mirage Hotel in Las Vegas was packed with over 16,000 people and by the time the match was over, and the decision was made, the crowd started to roar out boos. They were not pleased with the decision, but they all agreed "No Mas" or "No More" as the fight was titled.

Winning is something we all want to do, but sometimes we have to know when to say, "No Mas" and move to the next opponent or obstacle in life.

Fighting at Less than 100%

As an athlete, you're bound to get injured at some point and time, the question is when and how. That's something athletes are never prepared for. Who plans to get injured when your mind is focused on winning? As an amateur boxer, I train hard and long to prepare for tournaments. During this time nothing else matters to me but training. I get up early to train, I rest, eat, and train a second time until it's dark outside. I love it because I am knocking out my goals one by one.

If I am ever defeated in a match, it's because I was fighting less than 100%. During one of my bouts I threw a miscalculated jab and I felt intense pain. As soon as it was thrown, I knew something was wrong. Nonetheless, I knew I had to keep fighting. In your battles through life, pressing through feelings of "discomfort" just further proves that you are determined to overcome no matter what. Knowing when to quit is important. I have come to learn that it is ok to sit out to recover and to wait until you are in the proper headspace to win mentally and physically. I won with one injured hand, and it was a gamble. The hand injury I sustained that day during the fight was minimal. However, I was still injured, I just didn't know the extent of the injury until after the bout. I was asked if I wanted to proceed with the fight and I said, "yes, I can win with one hand," and I did. I did not gloat, I took the win and learned from things I could have done better.

There was another five-day tournament that I really wanted to compete in. I trained for months for this day and winning it was going to rank me higher as an amateur boxer. The first day of the tournament, after my opponent's elbow landed on my jab, I started to feel some discomfort, but I got through it and I won. Later that night I was feeling the after effects. I drove myself to the store to get Epsom salt and aspirin to reduce inflammation and minimize the pain. On day two of the tournament I decided to fight. My logic was, I had trained for months and prepared myself mentally; it was hard not to go on with the match. Needless to say, I did not win. I was disappointed for days, but I knew I couldn't stay in that negative headspace and had to face the choices I made landed me there. I further reflected on my decisions and just had to tell myself, "you did this." The question was, how was I going to learn from it and move forward? When you are a winner, you can look at yourself during these tough moments in your life and take all the accountability of what you did wrong and just learn from them. You may have lost the fight physically, but once you start to take ownership of the role you played in the hurdle, then you are a true champion and win mentally each time.

Contender's Corner

I know fear is not a factor for us champs, but we have to analyze our situations and make the best decisions, even if that means calling upon your corner men. As you can see, an injury can be the difference between winning and losing. This game is a thinking man's sport and no matter how strong you may in fact be, fighting while injured can cause more damage than it initially did and set you up to lose. This round we almost got taken out of the game for good. Even at this professional level, we have to remember that winning and losing both present growth opportunities in the long run.

Think about the questions below.

- Think about a time when you lost in a situation. What was your reaction? How did you feel?

- What adjustments did you not make to prevent the same mistakes from happening again?

- Now think about a time you won in a situation. What was your reaction? How did you feel?

- What were some things you could have done better to master a certain area for the next time?

A good champion always revaluates himself, no matter if they took home the W or L.

Round 11:

Following Instructions

"Always Do the Right Thing!"

"With experience in boxing, you learn how to be a scientific boxer and fight easy." -Mannny Pacquiao

Congratulations, you have gone pro!

You are so close to the title belt. Your professionalism is on point and I, not once, doubted your skills. That last round was not an easy one to swallow because what champion wants to lose, but your reaction to it all kept me positive of the champion you will become. As a boxer, you need to know your strengths and study the weakness of your opponents. This will allow you to strategize how to move to beat them.

This is the 11th round and we are within arm's length of reaching the championship. Please know that many people that started out on this voyage with you did not make it to the professional level of boxing. I can taste it, can you? Your goals are in plain view with your name in shiny gold letters on it. In life, many people will start the course with you and some will not finish because something in one of those rounds, they could not master. It does not mean they will not meet their goals, but it does mean they must work hard and re-strategize. You may ask, why I chose following directions for the next to last round. You may wonder why this was not mentioned sooner. The thought process is simple, following directions is something you will need to do for the rest of your life. No matter what level you get to in your career, following directions is imperative if you want to make it to the next. In and out of the ring there has to be a moral compass or guide that you follow to. As a young boxer, I have not always listened to the instructions of my team and it costs me something. See, when you do not follow instructions most of the time there is a cost, even if it is a minute cost, there is a price to pay. And this is in the ring as well as out of the ring. As a professional boxer, you will always be encouraged to follow instructions. I know sometimes when we get to a certain level or age in life, being "governed" by someone else to a degree is not favorable, but it is quite necessary. Do not get me wrong when I use "governed" I use it loosely to bring home an idea that there is always someone in your corner or life that can provide perspective that you have not even thought of. When you do not follow directions often times you learn unnecessary lessons or are hurt badly, physically and mentally. But when you do follow directions, even in unfavorable situations you come out the victor and you are able to continue the fight to greatness. Which side of the spectrum will you be on?

Do the Right Thing

Recollecting on a time that I followed directions really makes me uneasy. This is one of those unfavorable situations I mentioned earlier. Had I not done what was asked of me, this book would probably had read another way. The "what if's" are endless, but the lesson I learned this day and that I want you to realize that sometimes instructions are not fair or even feasible, but in those unfavorable situations do what you know is the appropriate decision to make in your personal life. Integrity like in round 8.

When I was 18 years old, just a few short years ago, I graduated from high school. This is a pivotal moment in people's lives because it commemorates the becoming an adult. I was excited and looking forward to the next years of my life and career as a boxer. I attended a few graduation parties and after my long day of celebrating and making memories with my friends and family, I decided to make an ATM deposit. I collected quite a bit of monetary gifts for my accomplishments that day, and the responsible thing to do was deposit them all. Still on a natural high off the events of my day, I stopped at the first free standing ATM machine to conduct my business. As I wrapped up my transaction, I tossed the deposit receipt in the trash and was met by five flashing squad cars and all the police officers jumped out. Immediately the line of questioning ensued, and I was told I fit the description of someone who had been breaking the encasing off ATM's. I was not asked what I was doing, I was instantly assumed to be the assailant. Oddly enough, I was already on the phone while I was at the ATM conducting my business, and they allowed me to call my mom and she arrived within five minutes. This particular ATM location was very close to our home. I quickly explained to her the situation over the phone and I stayed calm and collected through the entire ordeal. My father always taught me to remain calm in all situations including inside the ring. He said to never show fear or any emotions because at that moment, they have the upper hand. Once my mom arrived, she started freaking out like any concerned mom would. She later revealed that she was terrified!

The officers refused to let me talk to her once she arrived, and they even threatened to arrest the both of us if she didn't step back and stop talking. I showed them the receipt on my cell phone, to prove I had just made a deposit, but that was not good enough. I followed every instruction, so the dilemma would peacefully dissolve. We must have been there for over an hour going through the same story. One of the officers finally looked in the trash can, which I asked him to do earlier, and saw another receipt which showed that I in fact did just make a deposit. And just like that it was over. Through the entire process I was calm, and I realized that remaining that way and following those "unfavorable instructions", things did not escalate.

When facing situations in life, follow instructions even in those tough times. This story would have read differently had I not kept calm and did what was asked of me. Any sudden moves or deviating from the instructions given to me plain, would have not been a good outcome.

I can see the sweat in your brows. This round is up and the 12th round is now here. You have been trained well, and you will succeed.

Contender's Corner:

In chapter 10, we learned about winning and losing and when we made it here to this round, we learned how following directions are a direct reflection to winning. We have been working rigorously to get to this level of professionalism. I believe in you. You have worked through learning how a boxer moves through his journey to make it to the title belt and how you can apply these principles to your life to win.

Reflect on the following questions and think about your willingness to follow instructions.

- Think of a time when you did adhere to the instructions given to you. What lessons did you learn?

- Think of a time when you did not adhere to the instructions given to you. What did it cost you? What will you do differently next time?

- So far, what has been the most difficult area in your life to take instructions in? Why?

- What have you learned in these last 11 rounds that has prepared you the most for the 12th round when reaching your goals?

Round 12

Champion

"A Champion is Born"

"Anything you can complete mentally, you can complete physically." – Evan Holyfield

3:00

Congratulations is in order, you have endured to the end. This is it champ! This is what we have been working so diligently towards. The championship, the title belt, the bragging rights! All the training and coaching you have attained prepared you for this moment. It is either go big or go home. This round will be intense, but rest assured that you have all the tools you need to bring home the belt-- champ. There are a lot of people counting on you to win. No pressure, right? You made it to the pro level and there is no turning back now. Remember, many started with you, but only the strong fought through and made it here. My prediction for this round is an undefeated champion. When the seed of defeat starts to overtake your mind, the easiest and most logical thing to do is to quit, but we have moved past that stage. Think about what we learned in round five, your mindset is the key.

The clock is moving fast.

2:15

With blood, sweat, and determination in your eyes, keep your eyes on your goals and opponent to keep the passion burning inside of you. I know you are fatigued, I know your body aches, I know you feel like stopping, but we are almost there. So far, you have been getting through these rounds with a bit of struggle, but the most important thing is that you made it. Keep fighting and keep throwing those combo punches. There are hundreds of combinations you can muster up in one match. Your opponent is not going to give in that easily; you both made it to this final round and the road has not been a cake walk. I know you wanted to throw in the towel, but your grit, the true champion inside of you, kept you moving. I know your body feels like calling the match, but it will all pay off soon. Remember the story I shared with you about my personal runs up and down Stone Mountain, those runs can become grueling to me physically, even after I have convinced myself that I can do it. That is very challenging for me, especially when my legs feel like boulders. This is sort of what this last round is like, you already told your mind you can do it, but your body is screaming for you to surrender. The look in your eyes tells me your body will not win. The majority of the people would have quit in life and in the boxing ring, but you dug deep to finish what you started. Life is a series of small tests; will you make the grade? Remember your dreams and goals have no concern of how you feel, so despite the way you feel, your ironclad mindset must kick in and get you through this. Take it a step at a time, talk to yourself a little bit more, before you know it you have finished the round. Pain is temporary, because you only feel the pain if you ponder on it for too long. Tell yourself it does not hurt. Practice is harder than the real fight. All your practice prepared you for the fight. Ask God for strength and let's win this round.

Your skill never ceases to amaze me. You have taken all these principles and made them work for you. Any of your goals or future challenges do not stand a chance up against you. The difference of you losing the fight is by 15 or 20 seconds, the judges make the last decision. Make your punches count. Let us refresh your memory before the end of the fight...

Remember the clock is ticking. 11 Rounds under our belt.

- **Discipline** – Taught you that hard work, determination and sacrifice is needed to get you to this moment.

2:10

- **Sparring** – Prepares us for the fight so we can fine tune ourselves and correct our mistakes. Spar with other people who are striving to be great in life and in the boxing ring. This only makes you better, your goal is to always improve and the only way to improve is to spar with someone with a better skill set than you. Your skill set will help them advance as well. Sparring is all about give and take.

- **Circle** – Look around at the very people that have stuck with you on this journey and through your transformation, as a novice to a professional. Those people should be in your corner or your squad. These rounds served some unexpected let downs and some anticipated victories, through it all you needed those sound people to count on, so they could help you get a win. Make sure in life, when heading to your goals your "squad" want you to get that win.

2:00

- **Mindset** – Whatever you think you are, that is what you will become. We have already established that you are a winner. Keep powering through! Less than a minute left.

- **Accountability** – Always be responsible for YOU! Take ownership of what you have to complete. Your success is all up to you!

- **Pressure** – It will be applied, much like this championship round, but you can give it your best shot and put on a great performance. It is too late for jitters. Pressure makes diamonds!

1:35

- **Adversity** – You can fight through anything.

- **Integrity** – What you do when no one is looking is what counts!

- **Fear** – Never show fear because your opponent will take advantage of it. Any detection of weakness will jeopardize your outcome in the ring.

1:25

- **Winning & Losing** – No matter if you take home a L or a W, learn from it and get better.

- **Following Instructions** – Make sure you continue to follow instructions until the very end of the round. Mistakes, mishaps, and misunderstandings can be avoided. I'm excited, we are getting closer.

This is it champ; the clock is ticking.

1:15

Keep pushing, throw a left jab, your opponent/goal is weak on the left side.

0:59

Make each blow count, the bell is about to ring, your opponent/goal is getting fatigued. I see you are resting on your opponent/goal, trying to get seconds of rest, he is running out of gas too. All you have to do is keep fighting for a few more seconds. With your bruised eye and a single trickle of blood dripping down your face, I need you to find the strength to keep swinging. Make sure your swings count, they need to be accurate. Each swing you make puts you closer to achieving what you set out to achieve. Remember when we talked about the rope-a-dope, get your opponent on the ropes and make these jabs count. We are coming up to the bell. Pull out your powerful left uppercut and knock out your opponent/goal for the title belt!

You went through everything you went through, and you weathered the storm, at the end of this round, it's your choice to throw that last punch, it's your choice to win.

:00

DING, DING, DING! Win by way of knockout!

We did it, no, you did it! You are the champion and hold the title belt. Any goal, dream or accomplishment you desire to achieve will be seamless.

Contender's Corner:

You did it! Win by way of knock out!

You must always finish strong, in the ring and when moving towards you goals in life. Especially if the fight is close, if you can see the finish line, this is when you turn up your game, this is where what you worked for counts. It all comes down to those last seconds. When working hard to win, you have to always remember to remain calm. You have been equipped with all you need to be the winner. When the fight gets tough, this is when you show the goals/opponent who you are. When those goals in life look like a moving target, you have to give it your all. I would not mention this if you did not have to always consider it. The fight might be close, but your discipline, training, and heart will be the determining factor to the win. You would rather your opponent to run out of gas, than to sit there and lose and not do anything. However, in the fight, the judge makes the decisions, always keep that into account. Make the right decisions. Be precise in your delivery.

Consistency makes you successful. You do not earn this title as champion overnight. There is perseverance, sacrifice, hard-work, dedication, and passion that makes this happen. When you have all those things understood, you conclude that you will not let the opponent win. The other guy does not know how tired you are. Your goals do not care how you feel, but they have to be reached. Always keep that into account, in and out of the ring.

I'll leave you with this, in these 12 rounds to winning for the youth, I pray that you have found the inspiration and courage to start and/or keep striving towards your goals, no matter the odds stacked up against you. Every story that I shared was designed to provide the spirit of resilience and confidence through my personal life experiences, my father, my coaches and my knowledge for the sport of boxing.

Write down your goals and develop a plan based on what you have learned in this book. You have already won because you are a **CHAMPION**.

_____

_____

_____

_____

_____

_____

_____

_____

_____

About the Author

Amateur boxer, 20-year-old Evan Holyfield, lives in Atlanta, Georgia and has a deep passion for youth, philanthropy, and boxing. Being a young adult himself, he knows the importance of developing a winner's mindset at an early age. Evan started his boxing journey at eight years old. Evan grew up in a competitive environment all of his life, and his relentless desire to win keeps him motivated. When he is not perfecting his boxing craft, he is working a part-time job, or giving back to the community by participating in charity boxing matches, which benefit the youth. Holyfield is no stranger to volunteering his time at hospital's and homeless shelters to serve children and adults alike. Serving and giving to others has fervently been instilled in Evan at an early age and he continues to show his commitment of being a motivator and encourager to the youth. He is also the son of the four-time heavyweight champion of the world boxer, Evander Holyfield. His love of boxing was by no accident. Although Evan is creating his

Photo by Herman Rodriguez

own path in boxing, he will attest to the values his father has taught him.

Evan currently ranks #1 for the Georgia Golden Gloves. Evan's dream is to become a professional world champion boxer. Holyfield is passionate about teaching youth basic boxing skills while imparting discipline, sportsmanship and focus. He feels that the skills of boxing will assist kids in following their own dreams with a champion's mindset.

All historical facts were found on www.Wikipedia.com

Made in the USA
Lexington, KY
25 November 2019

57675867R00066